Maurizio Di Meo

A Million Euros

Title: A million Euros

Author: Maurizio Di Meo

Publisher: Lulu.com

Copyright: © 2008 Standard Copyright License

Language: Italian

Country: Italy

Version: First Edition

English translation by Antonio Siclari

Isbn :

INTRODUCTION

Forbes magazine has declared that an individual is defined rich, when he has an annual income of a million dollars and a net property of ten million dollars. Well, I will teach you how to earn your first million Euros.

We live in an era in which too much little time and too much information are in competition among them. If we want to realize our aims, we need new abilities to select, elaborate and learn new information.

Through some histories of real life, my friend Flavio's one, who is millionaire today. Techniques, that will help to let the millionaire that is in you to emerge, and some tolls will let you get a really free person. Free financially. And when you will be getting it, you can say goodbye to your actual job. Pay attention, I don't mean that it will be an easy way; however I can tell you that, with a little of care at the end all we can get millionaire.

THE BEGINNING

The first thing to be done is to totally change your approach toward the rich people. Since we are children, we grow with the conviction that the rich persons are avid and despicable people, who think only to get richer and richer. We hear sentences like: *"That guy has become wealthy defrauding the poor people"* or *"All the money that he has is accursed"* and still *"He has so much money to turn my stomach"*, and so on. It is not this way. The rich people deal a lot with beneficence, and they do it in silence, (the most of them), not by the first pages of the newspapers.

We are workers' children, we were born poor, and we have grown with the conviction that money is the evil of the society. We have always associated the money to the evil. It is true, there are some people that have illegally become wealthy, but they are an almost invisible minority. A very rich friend of mine, Flavio (name of imagination): "If you want to become really rich, you have to LOVE THE

MONEY, you have to love the rich people and learn from them.

He also says that it is so easy to honestly earn money that is not worth to risk to go to the jail.

THE ATTITUDE

To change your mental state, your attitude in the life of every day in the way of facing the things, the business, the investments, it is the first step toward the wealth.

Listening to these words, the first sentences that you think of are <<Will it be impossible to me to earn a million of Euros starting from zero? >> And more, <<If I earn thousand Euros a month, with all the expenses that I have, it will be really impossible to earn a million of Euros>> Well, it is just this your problem! From now on, try to change these sentences with <<How can I do, starting from zero, to earn a million of Euros? >> or <<Today I earn thousand Euros a month, how can I change this situation, considering all the expenses that I have?>> Well, this is a correct attitude toward the wealth.

You have to cancel the word *impossible* from your dictionary. Anything you want to do, or you have thought about doing, start cancelling the word IMPOSSIBLE from your dictionary and replace it with I CAN or HOW I CAN today to change my situation.

When we have a new idea, we immediately think that it is the good time, we talk about it to our relatives, colleagues, friends and we introduce our winning idea to all them. After having exposed with clarity our idea, convinced that it is the good one and it will make us enrich, everything will start.... but, if it doesn't go how you think, but if this doesn't happen, but with all the authorizations that are needed. And it is just at this point that we begin to discourage, and we see so many doubts in our mind appearing. Our look begins to change, and the fear to fail crosses our whole body. At the end of the presentation the only thing that you will say really convinced is <<You are perhaps right. It will be a failure>>.

"Our doubts are traitors, and they make us lose the good that we could get because we are afraid to try."

(William Shakespeare)

THE FRIEND FLAVIO

My friend, Flavio, was born by a poor family, his dad was a building worker, he was born in province in the south, he has left the school when he was 16 years old, and went to work with an agricultural cooperative, and his task was to load the trucks with boxes of fruit. Later around one year, he changes job and does the same for the following five years. He had changed many kinds of job, between one and the other; he started understanding that to be dependent doesn't suit him. Flavio liked very much reading. In these five years he has read everything till when he heard about PNL < <neuro linguistic planning>> founded by Richard Bandler in the seventies.

(The PNL teaches to develop practice of success, amplifying the easy behaviours and decreasing the undesirable ones. The change can happen reproducing with attention the behaviours and the beliefs of the people of success. The

PNL sustains that the people possess in themselves all the resources to be successful).

Since then, his attitude toward the life begins to change, he is very more optimist, very self confident. On an economy book, he read a thing that impressed him very much: the 80/20 rule, invented by the Italian economist Vilfredo Pareto. In few words the 80% of our success is coming from the 20% of our efforts. For many people today it is still the contrary instead, the effort of the 80% produces a 20% of success to them. By these small inputs, the walk toward the change of Flavio started. He looked back, he thought about all the sacrifices that his father had done in his life, to his sacrifices up to that moment, to fruit's boxes on the trucks that seemed to never end. And just in that very instant Flavio said: <<My life will be plenty for me, for my family and for all the people that I can help. I will get the financial freedom. I won't depend on the job anymore for the money, but the money will work for me. >>

There was here the real turn point in Flavio's life.

For you that are reading this book, the moment of your turning point has come.

Can you imagine your life plenty? In the comfort? A life that goes over your salary?

I just think so; otherwise you would not have bought this book.

"Make the first step with faith. It doesn't need that you see the whole staircase, it is enough that you start going up on the first stair."

(Martin Luther King Jr)

THE TARGETS

Fix some targets and follow them with determination and constancy.

Start with some small targets; write them down, day by day. Doing so, you will fix them in your mind and, step by step, you will get the top of your financial range. Don't limit yourself to read them with a loud voice, but write them again on a sheet. This is a Brian Tracy's idea. He concentrates mentally every day on what he wants to realize in that day, and he writes it down. When you are writing a target, think only about what you want, and never to what you don't. Imagine how much you will be happy to see your targets come true. Imagine the money that you will earn for every target you get.

The targets have not to be a torment. Example: if you have to make a drastic diet to lose 15 kilos, what do you do? Do you eat fruit and vegetable, till when you don't get your target? No, because it will be a torment. To get your ideal weight, your target, goes to a physician, who will prescribe you a balanced diet for your organism. Following the diet every day, it will be a big sacrifice for you, but only for the first ten or fifteen days, till when you won't have gotten used, then you will follow the diet in a totally and automatic way. And the same thing happens with the money, once that you have gotten used to have it, it will always arrive more and more automatically. Earning money is like riding a bicycle. The first time one falls, then one falls again, then we get up and we fall again, till when we automatically ride it, without even thinking that we are on a bicycle. It becomes a habit. Here it is: to be rich is a habit.

Then, as regards your financial position, you need a physician, a money physician, one who teaches you to resolve your financial problems and become millionaire.

THE PHYSICIAN OF YOUR MONEY

First of all, you need a money physician, practically a mentor, he who is today already, where you would like to be tomorrow. A person from whom you can get a myriad of information, expert in investments, who is already millionaire, and therefore he can suggest you only the best to make you get your financial freedom. Pay attention not to confuse the mentor with a financial advisor or a banker, he is totally an autonomous person, a holder enterprise, an investor. The financial advisor, the banker, also being very educated people, they are and they will be always some employees, they will always give you the same answers: "Invest in a common fund for your old age" or "Purchase some long-term state funds". If you will keep on listening to their suggestions, you won't do anything else but make their game, and keep on being poor. You have done the first step toward the wealth, purchasing this book. When you are at the end of the book, you will be also at the end of the tunnel of the poverty, at the end of the tunnel you will begin to see the light, you will have some small opening of light toward your financial freedom. If you are thinking about asking for loan to a mentor, be sure that none of your mentor will lend you some money, because if they will do it, they will make you only poorer. However, at the moment in which you are ready to invest, and you will have an affair that will make you ear some money of 20% at least, in a relatively short time, the mentor won't lend you the money for the operation, but he will invest them with you. My mentor has been Flavio and in his turn he has had a mentor.

We generally think that <<if you want a job doing, do it yourself>>, but fortunately it is not this way.

THE TEAM

If you want to become really rich, you need a team: (better if not relatives so you can reproach them in the moment they don't do their job well)

a lawyer,

a professional accountant,

a bank clerk,

just to start, then according to the job that you carry out, you will engage some professional men in the sector.

To make you understand the importance of a team, I tell you what happened to Henry Ford in the epoch of the industrial era. He has been one of the greatest businessmen in the world, he become rich realizing the saying of his firm, the Ford Motor Company. *"Democratize the car"*, this was his saying. He was so revolutionary, because at the beginnings of 1900, the car was only within the reach of some rich men. Well, Ford's idea was to try to that all everyone could allow themselves a car. After having drawn his first car, in 1903 he founds the FORD MOTOR COMPANY. Starting from nothing, he began to build his first car, with his team, his obstinacy and his desire to get the financial freedom, in little time he founded a motor empire. He has not only allowed everybody could have a car, but he even paid the highest salaries of the sector. In few words, Henry Ford became rich because he cared about his clients, and also his workers. He was a generous man! He was not educated, and he was often criticized by the so called big brains of the academic world. One day they proposed him to take an examination, to try him out, he accepted. In the day and at the fixed time, some big brains went to his office, and they immediately started with the first question <<Mr. Ford can you tell us what is the resistance to the traction of the steel used by you?>> Ford, that didn't know the answer, phoned to the vice-president (the TEAM). After few minutes, the vice-president came in, Ford asked him the question and he answered, giving the answer that all wanted to hear. Then, they asked another question to Ford and he phoned again to another person (the TEAM) of his staff who gave the answer that all wanted. And so they kept on, till when one of them got up, and said, "Mr. Ford this shows that you are ignorant". He replied, this time. "Look Mr… I don't know the answers because I cannot stuff my head to give the answers to You. I engage clever people that do it for me. My job is to keep my head free to be able to think". And while he was inviting the people to go out, he said "Thinking is the hardest job that exists. This is the reason why so few people you they devote themselves to it".

And you, what you have to do now, it is to think about your cash flow. In my opinion, it is really the first thing to be done.

CASHFLOW

Is your cash flow produced by your job or by your investments today?

To get rich you have take the control of your cash flow.

You have to consider your finances and your household budget like a big firm, with incomes, outcomes, credits and debits. For this reason it is fundamental to draft a personal financial account. Draw up your financial account, and you can exactly understand where you are today. If you are an employee, your gross income, today it is around 1700 Euros a month, (middle salary of an Italian government employee with wife and two children to provide). Then your financial account could be this way:

Profit and loss account

Income   Outcome

Salary	1700,00	Loan Instalment	400,00
	0	Car Instalment	100,00
	0	Food stuff	400,00
	0	School	150,00
	0	Bills	100,00
	0	Taxes	450,00
	0	Various	100,00
Tot. Income	1700	Tot. Outcome	1700

Financial standing

Active   Passive

	0	Loan Instalment	400,00
	0	Car Instalment	100,00
	0		0
	0		0
	0		0

Your cash flow is zero. It is just here your financial problem: the cash flow.

It is not important how much income you can produce, but how much you can keep creating further incomes, and therefore furthering cash flow.

Many people, employees and non ones, are in this situation. The most of the people don't manage their own financial account; at best they try to balance accounts every month.

Have you drawn up your financial account?

Draw it up!

Well done! You are a step forward in comparison with your colleagues.

At the beginning of this chapter, I have told you to consider your life like a great firm. As administrators of your firm (life) you have not to do anything else but checking the incomes and the losses. You always have to remember that yours liabilities are credits for somebody else. In this case the interest of your loan instalment of 400,00 € and the instalment for your car of 100,00 € are earning for your bank. You are working very hard get your bank richer. What you have to do instead, it is to enrich yourselves, first of all.

Every month, with a small sacrifice, start saving the 10% of your incomes, put them aside, for the time being in a not tied up fund, start hoarding, you have to go up the staircase step by step, do you remember? You absolutely have to go out of the wheel of the hamster. You turn and turn, but you go nowhere. It is the system that is wrong. Even if your salary was 3400,00 Euros a month, the cash flow would be always zero. It is a matter of mentality, of habit to manage the money at the best. With a higher income, you would make only enrich the others more. You will purchase a bigger house, a more beautiful car, a new scooter, a little flat at the seaside and so on, until make your cash flow get zero. The column of the liabilities would be even longer, and you won't have done anything else but increasing the earning of your bank. It has come the moment to say : <<STOP! STOP! STOP! From now on I will draw up my financial account every month, always setting aside the 10% of my earnings, I will check all my debts and I will pay them off, one by one. I won't have bad debts anymore, but only good debts.>>

GOOD DEBTS - BAD DEBTS

The good debts are all those that produce a positive cash flow. If you contract a loan for the purchase of an immovable property to rent, and this produces a positive cash flow, between the difference of the loan instalment and the rent that you receive, this is a good debt. Example: loan of 70000 Euros, loan instalment of 400 Euros, rent of 500Euros. Well this operation has a positive cash flow of 100 Euros a month. Instead, returning to the previous example, to the chart of your financial account, the loan instalment of 400 Euros is a bad debt. I explain you why. In Italy the most of us grow with the conviction that the first thing to be done, when one has a decent job "the good job", it is to purchase the house for one's own family, and this is just the mistake. Buying the house where you live is not an investment: it is a wrong thing by the financial point of view. If you use your possibility of indebtedness with a bank to purchase the house where you live, instead of purchasing a house to resell or rent, you cannot produce more money. That investment doesn't produce cash flow, it doesn't produce money flow in your pockets and therefore, it is not an investment but a cost! A cost that you pay for 15, 20, 30 years... as long as your loan lasts! If you use your ability of indebtedness instead to purchase a house that you rent, money comes in your pockets as an income. This is a right immovable investment. And it doesn't matter that so you don't pay the rent: if you invest in immovable properties it is right to pay the rent for the house where you live. The most of the investors in immovable properties do this way, I do this way. I preserve my ability of indebtedness to make it work, not to pay a roof on my head.

Today you have to invest in immovable properties to get real money: when you will have got them sufficiency, you can buy the house that you desire, even cash.

Remember: <<Economic independence is reached improving our own abilities, earning well and finally not wasting the money>>.

One of the methods to quickly get rich is the trading of immovable properties.

INVESTING IN IMMOVABLE PROPERTIES

My friend Flavio has begun to invest in immovable properties when he was 21 years old. He found a flat to restructure, next to the university centre. It was on sale for 100 million liras (at that time there was the lira in Italy, today a Euro is worth 1936,27 liras), practically 52000 Euros today. Flavio made a proposal of 35000 Euros and it was refused. They finally agreed for 40000 Euros, 35000 Euros by a loan and 5000 Euros by an annual promissory note. He had no money and guarantees to give to the bank. Then he proposed the affair to some friends of his that had a paypacket, and they went to the bank to contract a loan. Once got the flat, Flavio and company immediately started restructuring it. Once the word finished, Flavio rents the four rooms to the students creating a positive cash flow of 250 Euros. But Flavio's aim was to resell the flat which, thanks to the restructuring works and the income of the students, got the value of 95.000 Euros. Once they sold the flat, Flavio and his two friends, paying all the expenses, pocket

10.000 Euros each. Well done, considering that at that time, in order to earn 10.000 Euros (around 20 millions liras) they would have taken more than one year of hard work. Well, Flavio has become rich this way. One of the last Flavio's investments, it has been the one to purchase an immovable property of 4000 square meters, on four floors, for a total of 2.400.000 Euros. Restructured and divided in 60 unities of 60 squared meters each, more common spaces, with an expense of 1.600.000 Euros. He has resold each flat 2.000 Euros for square meter; 120.000 Euros each with a gross proceed of 7.200.000 Euros. I let you to make the calculation of Flavio's net gain in this operation.

Obviously you cannot start investing million of Euros, however you can begin purchasing a studio flat, then a small flat, a small villa and who knows, an immovable property of 4000 square meters one day.

I don't say that it is simple; at the beginning you could also check 300 properties before finding 30 of them that can be a business for you. Of these, perhaps, the half deserves an inspection. Finally on 15 properties it will be really worth to make an offer for three or four of them only. The offer will always have to be less than 30%.

Buying at a discount is possible. There are the auctions by Court order, the bankruptcy ones; there are all those people that must get rid of an immovable property because of many reasons (transfers, job, inheritance to be divided, etc.). In this case we can play on the element time so that to reduce even more marginally the price to our advantage.

Don't lose heart; think the profit that you can get at the end of the operation. You are on the way of the financial freedom.

An article published by "Il Sole 24 ore", last April told: <<The influence of the summer crisis of the American loans, the dear-loans of the last months and the prices of the houses always so expensive are trying the real estate market, Italian one too. Away from the serious American estate crisis, for the trading of the residential compartment in our Country, one cannot speak of collapse yet. But of a re-evaluation surely>>. What are you thinking? That this is not the moment to invest in immovable properties? You are wrong. There has been never more favourable period of this to invest in immovable properties.

Create some automatic income, so that they can produce you cash flow some without your material presence. Reinvest your earnings in immovable properties to rent and produce further cash flow. This way you can get rich.

A villa like this could be yours one day. You can get it only by making the money work for you and not you work for the money.

THE SYSTEM

Today we are passed from Henry Ford's industrial era to the Bill Gates' information era. What really counts today is to have a system.

Around the turn of 1800 and 1900, not long after than one hundred years ago, the most of the population was independent farmers or little merchants. Only a little percentage of the population was composed by employees. Then with the coming of the industrial era - the promise of a sure and well remunerated work and the safety to have a good old age pension - the most of the farmers and the dealers gave up the independence and got some employees. And since then, from the epoch of the industrial era that we hand down from father to son the idea of the sure work. The accomplice of all this was our scholastic system, planned for creating employees and professional men, not entrepreneurs or investors.

I guess that you know how to make a hamburger better than Mc Donald's, isn't it?

Well, how come does Mc Donald's sell million of hamburger and French fries, every day, in every place of the earth?

It is not only the quality of the product to make you sell, but it is the system. It is the system that makes you become rich. When you have a system, you same some time, energy and money.

Ray Kroc, the Mc Donald's founder, has told once to some students of a master in business management, which his company was not in the sector of the hamburgers, on the contrary in the immovable one. In fact the Mc Donald's is owner of the most expensive immovable properties in the world. With the system that he had created, it allowed him to create some credits that produced other credits.

Warren Buffett, one of the greatest investors in the world, said <<Only two ways exist for producing comfort: finding a value, or creating it>>

Well, find what people want and try to make them have it.

Today in the era of the information, of internet, of the network marketing, everyone I say really everyone, can become millionaire.

If your idea is to sell a product, on line, by internet, it is what million of people make today. However, only few of them become millionaire. Why?

Because if you want to be successful in any sector you have to have a plan first, to fix what your goals are, whom you are addressing to and by what system you want to undertake the activity.

THE ACTION

I want to tell you a story, one of those told by my friend Flavio that has struck me very much. In 1980, in Irpinia there was a devastating earthquake, many people lost their life and a lot of houses were destroyed. Among these ones, the house of a poor family, till then, a poor but happy family. The father Vincenzo was a worker, the mother Alina was a housewife and they had got five children, two of them attended secondary school, while three were pre-school age. The father Vincenzo lost his life under the debris. Alina was always an optimistic woman, lively, but in that moment, by losing her husband, she felt herself lost. She felt the sky tumbling down, she felt like pushed by this big rock, which was her life without her husband, alone with five children. She had got no relations; she was coming from the Eastern countries and she move to Italy to get married with Vincenzo. After this tragedy, she started living with her children into one of the containers that the town council gave to the homeless persons. To feed her children, Alina started working. She was a chambermaid for a time. But she had the problem with her children that were so little, and she could not leave them to anybody, so she started doing house works. She assembled some toys for a north company, and she got a percentage for the work done. Alina, after some time, understood that more she worked, more she earned. The older sons helped her to assemble the toys, and more they did, more they earned. At a certain point, a flash came into Alina's head, and she said << If others do it, why can't I do too? >>.

Here it is Alina's optimism coming out. She thought to have some people doing the work she was doing with the toys till that moment, but with some jewellery. She started sending hundreds of letters to as many families, explaining which kind of work they had to do and how much money they could earn for each assembled piece of them. Also, if a person would have found other persons to have jewellery assembled, she promised a further earning on the work of these referral persons. She would have got only some gain for her, but can you imagine about on how much quantity? The marketing. Alina was only doing marketing. Well, Alina, by this method, sold million of pieces, by a simple idea she got her financial freedom. Alina is living with her children in her native country today. She sold her company several years ago, and she lives on a private income of her immovable properties.

I have told you this story in order you can realize that, sometimes, it is enough a simple idea to get rich.

There is no need to have got money to get more money.

It's not even true that to get mo/re money we have to work more and more, remember the rule well if you want to get money, you have to be part of that 20%.

The moment to act has come, any idea you have, in any sector, cancel your worries. Worries are the main danger for our health, happiness, success and try to put it in practice. You have to put apart even the fear to fail. Even the richest men in the world failed one time in their whole life. Donald Trump failed one time. Remember the example of the bike, after several attempts, and after some falls, you have to automatically pedal. The same is with all day life, business and money.

One has to act in the moment when you have got an idea and you feel it is the right one. Try to talk about it with other persons, with your relations and friends that you think they can be good employees, try to talk about with your "weak" connections.

Your relations, your friends, persons by whom you have always shared everything are your strong connections. They are all the people that were on the same wavelength as you, the persons by which you could talk about football, "dependent" work, dinners, holiday, but you could never talk about enterprise, immovable, interest rate, shares and so on. Well, these are your weak connections, and if you want to get rich, you will have to cultivate your weak connections.

THE TENTH PART

The richest persons in the world are benefactors. They always give the 10% of their income and earnings to charitable institutions.

This is the tenth part.

If you ask to some of these persons why one has to pay the tenth part, they will tell you that paying the tenth part always gives a good back in economic words about their own investments.

Giving means to extend and increase the money.

So many persons have an awareness marked by poverty, and they think that living money means to reduce the quantity at their disposal. For millionaires it is not so. They think that distributing money in charity, it means to extend the spiritual dimension, but it means to increase in exponential way their income.

When we take a fruit from a tree, nature will provide to give us two fruits at the same point.

That's how the tenth part works.

Have you ever heard about the saying << The more you give, the more you get >>.

The globalization makes the social differences increase, but it makes thousands new millionaires, ready to undertake in charity. There are about 9,5 millionaires in the world today. The 11% of these super rich men in 2006 gave more than 285 billion dollars, in other words about the 10% of their fortune.

So, start giving your part of earnings, and one day you will be listed in those statistics.

CONCLUSIONS

Remember to have a mentor, a team, and the most important thing, in my opinion; if you are tired to be a dependent, you have to change your attitude against the money, the wealth, people and life.

I have followed Flavio's advice. And you?

When you have some free time, don't waste it. Read PNL books, success persons' autobiography, look for new people, persons that can advise you and not demoralize you.

By this little advice, I hope to have helped you to go in for your way toward the financial freedom.

GOOD LUCK !

TABLE OF CONTENTS

INTRODUCTION 5

THE BEGINNING 6

THE ATTITUDE 8

THE FRIEND FLAVIO 10

THE TARGETS 13

THE PHYSICIAN OF YOUR MONEY 15

THE TEAM 17

CASHFLOW 20

GOOD DEBTS - BAD DEBTS 24

INVESTING IN IMMOVABLE PROPERTIES 26

THE SYSTEM 30

THE ACTION 33

THE TENTH PART 37

CONCLUSIONS 39

www.ingramcontent.com/pod-product-compliance
Lightning Source LLC
Chambersburg PA
CBHW021941170526
45157CB00005B/2377